W9-BBX-393

HUMAN BIOLOGY

Please visit our web site at: www.garethstevens.com
For a free color catalog describing Gareth Stevens Publishing's list of high-quality books and multimedia programs, call 1-800-542-2595 (USA) or 1-800-387-3178 (Canada). Gareth Stevens Publishing's fax: (414) 332-3567.

Library of Congress Cataloging-in-Publication Data

Human biology.
p. cm. — (Discovery Channel school science: the plant and animal kingdoms)
"First published in 2000 as Alive: the human biology files, by Discovery Enterprises, LLC, Bethesda, Maryland"—T.p. verso.
Summary: Explains what the human body is made of, how it works, what new discoveries are being made, and more.
ISBN 0-8368-3214-0 (lib. bdg.)
1. Human biology—Juvenile literature. [1. Human biology. 2. Body, Human.] I. Title. II. Series.
QP37.H887 2002
612—dc21 2002024505

This edition first published in 2002 by
Gareth Stevens Publishing
A World Almanac Education Group Company
330 West Olive Street, Suite 100
Milwaukee, WI 53212 USA

Further resources for students and educators available at www.discoveryschool.com

Designed by Bill SMITH STUDIO
Project Editors: Justine Ciovacco, Lelia Mander, Sharon Yates, Anna Prokos
Designers: Nick Stone, Sonia Gauba, Bill Wilson, Darren D'Agostino, Joe Bartos, Dmitri Kushnirsky
Photo Editors: Jennifer Friel, Scott Haag
Art Buyers: Paula Radding, Marianne Tozzo
Gareth Stevens Editor: Alan Wachtel
Gareth Stevens Art Director: Tammy Gruenewald

Printed in the United States of America

1 2 3 4 5 6 7 8 9 06 05 04 03 02

Writers: Jackie Ball, Stephen Currie, Dan Franck, John-Ryan Hevron, Susan W. Lewis, Chana Stiefel, Diane Webber, Christina Wilsdon, Sharon Yates

Editor: Sharon Yates

Photographs: Cover and p.2, rock climber, © Brian Bailey/TSI; p.2, soccer player, © Karan Kapoor/TSI; p.3, Globe, © MapArt; p.3, microscopic photo, © Quest /Science Photo Library/Photo Researchers, Inc.; pp.4-5, soccer player, © Karan Kapoor/TSI; p.6, brain, © Fred Hossler/Visuals Unlimited; p.10, microscopic photo, © Quest /Science Photo Library/Photo Researchers, Inc.; p.10, duodenal villi, Professor P. Motta /Dept. of Anatomy/University "La Sapienza," © Roma/Science Photo Library; p.11, microscopic photo, © Quest /Science Photo Library/Photo Researchers, Inc.; p.12, rock climber, © Brian Bailey/TSI; p.14, J. Krakauer, © Linda M. Moore; p.16, heart, © David Gifford/Science Photo Library/Photo Researchers, Inc.; p.16, © William Harvey, American Museum of Natural History/Special Collections; p.17, © Claudius Galen, Brown Brothers, Sterling, PA; p.22, organs, © Royal Collection, Windsor, England/A.K.G., Berlin/SuperStock; p.23, © Dr. Michael DeBakey, Baylor College of Medicine; p.25, Christopher Reeve, courtesy of Witeck Combs; p.26, biofeedback, © Will and Deni McIntyre/Photo Researchers, Inc.; p.28, Karen Olness, courtesy of Shawn Nemeth/University Hospitals of Cleveland; p.30, couple, © Dover Books; p.30, human body, © PhotoDisc; all other photographs, © COREL.

Illustrators: pp.18-19, Scott MacNeill; pp.26-27, Ron Tanovitz

Acknowledgments: pp.8-9, Lt. Kevin Malley, Director, Human Performance, New York City Fire Department; pp.14-15, excerpted from INTO THIN AIR by Jon Krakauer, Villard Books, NY, © 1997; p.17, Activity, data courtesy of Cooper Institute.

Up Close and Raring to Go

Ever have one of those days? Not the kind where you drag yourself out of bed, but one where you wake up feeling good, happy, full of energy, and almost tingly with anticipation for the day to begin? You feel you could do almost anything—swim a mile, climb a mountain, hit a homer. You're alive! And it feels great.

Fortunately, you don't need to check out all your body systems to see if they're working before getting out of bed. They work automatically. Perhaps this is why we don't think about our body systems. In HEALTH, Discovery Channel gives you the chance to find out some fascinating things about your body. For example, your powerful brain is about the size of a grapefruit, you breathe in about 23,000 times a day, and there's a whole lot of activity that goes on in the night while you're asleep. You'll also find out what the body's made of, how it works, what new discoveries are being made about it, and much more.

Just turn the page and begin to discover what's happening inside you right now!

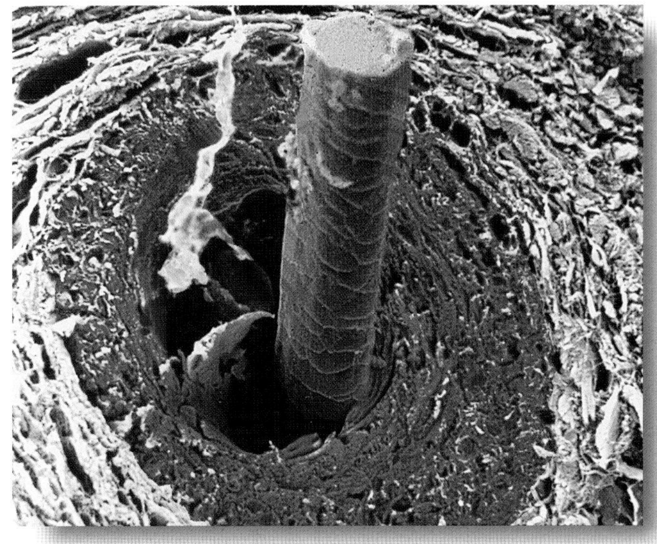

Can you guess what this is?...
See page 10

AT-A-GLANCE

Human Biology

The human body is a marvel of biology. The muscular-skeletal system, the endocrine system, the digestive, nervous, urinary, and other systems all work together to keep an individual alive. If you were to make a list of all the different jobs the human body does, you'd have a very long list, indeed. Eating, sleeping, smelling, thinking, running, breathing, laughing, and learning are just a few. The human body can also defend and repair itself when it is ill or injured. And it can reproduce. What's even more amazing is that the body does so many of these complex jobs simultaneously! No machine we've invented comes close to duplicating what the human body can do.

At the controls is the brain, masterminding the body's activities both when we're awake and when we're asleep. It's a good thing the brain does this. Imagine if you had to think about breathing every minute, or contracting your heart all the time, or blinking your eyes. No one could keep up with it all. Even if you could, you'd be so busy monitoring your body's functions, you wouldn't be able to do anything else.

Perhaps the most amazing characteristic of the human body is that it's both similar to and different from every other human body on Earth. Although all people have biological systems that work the same way, every body is unique.

BRAIN—The brain is the master controller of the nervous system and all your other systems. It receives and processes data about all parts of your body. It directs your body's responses. The brain does all this using electrical impulses that travel along the nervous system.

EYES—The eyes are part of the nervous system. They see all kinds of data about your surroundings and the path you are taking, then send the data to your brain.

Heart—You need extra energy when you're active. Your heart and circulatory system respond by pumping and delivering more blood, loaded with oxygen, to your muscles.

Lungs—The lungs and respiratory system bring fresh oxygen to your body. When you're active, your lungs and heart work harder but also grow stronger and more efficient. This means they can do their jobs better with less effort, making you stronger and healthier.

Muscles and Bones—The muscular and skeletal systems work together to support your weight, let you move, and power your stride.

Q & A

Gray Matters

Q: State your name, please.
A: Brain. B-R-A-I-N. First name, Human. What's going on?

Q: Suppose you tell us. We have top-level information that you're a fraud. According to our intelligence, you're a machine—one so extraordinary that no technology on Earth could have invented you. There's only one possible conclusion: Hostile aliens have sent you to take over the planet by controlling every human being on it.
A: Oh, come, come. It's true some call me a miracle. And I do control human bodies. But honestly, would anyone deliberately design a machine that looks like me?

Q: Well, we did wonder about that. Most machines are sleek and streamlined, not lumpy and gray and wrinkled. But that homely disguise could be part of a diabolical plan. At any rate, how can you be so small and do so much if you aren't a machine? Why, you're no bigger than a coconut.
A: Actually, a grapefruit is the usual comparison.

Q: And you couldn't weigh any more than an eggplant.
A: Again, closer to the weight of a head of cabbage. I don't want to be rude, but your powers of observation could use some sharpening. Anyway, I may look small, but humans have the largest brain size, compared to body size, of all land mammals. And even though I make up only two percent of an average body's weight, I need twenty percent of the body's total energy to keep working.

Q: Aliens sucking human resources dry! What better proof that you ARE a machine, and a wasteful one at that!
A: But I need all that power. Nothing works as hard at as many tasks as I do. I never stop.

Q: How about when humans are asleep, as they are a third of their lives?
A: How about it? Means nothing to me. I keep right on working: controlling breathing, heartbeat, digestion, making dreams, stuff like that. Some parts of the body don't shut down when the lights go out, you know. During the day, it's nonstop, directing every little

movement, keeping track of every little twitch and poke and tickle.

Q: So how do you do all that? What ARE you made of?
A: Tissue. Blood. About a hundred billion neurons. Those are nerve cells, ya know. But I don't do everything myself. I have some help—connections, you might call them.

Q: Accomplices! Other aliens!
A: No. It's just a system of nerves, and I'm at the center. We all work together.

Q: How do you all work together?
A: Through electricity.

Q: Aha! See? You ARE a machine!
A: Not through copper wires. Biological electricity. The billions of nerve cells in the brain, spinal cord, and nerves are all linked together in a huge network. Tiny electrical nerve signals are constantly carrying messages along that network.

Q: What kinds of evil secrets do you communicate with your allies?
A: Anything. Everything. Trillions of important and not-so-important things. Different parts of the body are always reporting things to me, and I have to figure out the best response. For instance, the body says it feels too hot. What do I do?

Q: I don't know. Say, I thought I was asking the questions!
A: Sorry, but I'm used to taking charge. The answer is that I send a message telling the sweat glands to get busy and cool things off. Or the nose says it itches, and I command a hand to scratch it. Or the body takes itself to a sad movie, and I mention to the tear ducts that it's time to overflow—but try not to get the popcorn soggy. When you think about it a certain way, it's the rest of the body that's the real commander. I'm at its service 24/7. That's the way it's always been.

Q: Since when? Since you were built?
A: I wasn't "built" all at once. I've been evolving for five hundred million years. At the beginning, I was only a brain stem, which is the total amount of brain reptiles have. That's why some scientists call my stem our "reptile brain." In reptiles, it devotes most of its energy to smells. In humans, it controls the real basics of being alive—breathing and heart rate. My biggest part is the cerebrum, which is divided into two sides called hemispheres. The left hemisphere controls the right side of the body and vice versa.

Q: What's the wrinkly gray stuff on top?
A: That's called the cortex. Some people call it gray matter. It wraps around the inside parts and it controls sensing and moving. It's also a nice protective layer. And surrounding the cortex, of course, is a rock-solid cage of bone called the skull.

Q: All right—one last question: is there anything you can't do?
A: Sure. Since I started developing hundreds of millions of years ago, when life was very different, sometimes I get overloaded with noise or overcrowding or too many sensations at one time—the problems of modern life. That's when I can stress out, and since I'm connected to all the other systems, that can cause illness or other physical problems.

Q: So, are you saying you're an obsolete machine?
A: Not at all. I can never be obsolete, because I'm as unique as the person whose body I inhabit. But I'm human, like those bodies. You can't fix me with any old spare part. And, besides, I repeat, would I look like this if I were designed on purpose?

Activity

SIZE WISE The human brain is just 2 percent of an average person's body weight. Choose 10 animals and do some research to find out their brain size and average body weight. Make a graph of your findings. Is there any relationship that you can figure out between brain and body size? Can you draw any conclusions about brain size and behavior?

TIMELINE

SYSTEMS UNDER FIRE!

One eventful hour in the life of a firefighter can involve every major muscle group and almost every system of the body. Lt. Kevin Malley, the director of human performance for New York City's fire department, calls firefighters "industrial athletes" because they need to be in great physical shape to do their jobs safely. Lt. Malley describes the physical and mental challenges a firefighter must deal with in the imaginary scenario below.

4:10 a.m.
The alarm sounds. Firefighter Johnson hears the bell and bolts out of bed. His brain directs the release of adrenaline into his system, making him more alert more quickly. He uses his senses of sight and touch to locate his gear. And he uses his memory, which is also sharpened by adrenaline, to make sure he has everything he needs with him.

4:12 a.m.
He slides down the pole and dashes to the truck.

4:15 a.m.
On the way to the fire, Johnson and the rest of Ladder Co. 123 hear, over the radio, that it is a two-alarm blaze, and someone is trapped. As Johnson wonders what he will find there, his pulse quickens, and his breathing gets faster.

4:18 a.m.
On the scene, Johnson and the rest of his company size up the situation: fire on the fourth floor of an apartment building. Johnson will lead the search team. He and his team sprint toward the building. Running on level ground, they are propelled mainly by the muscles of their lower legs.

4:19 a.m.
Running up the stairs, Johnson's upper leg muscles do most of the work. Equipment and protective clothing add 68 pounds to his 175-pound frame.

4:21 a.m.
Johnson reaches the fire floor, breathing heavily. He has to get down on all fours because it is very smoky. It's time to start breathing through his respirator. He knows from experience that, at his current rate of exertion, he has about 15 minutes of air in the tank he carries on his back.

4:22 a.m.
He can hear someone screaming in the apartment, but the front door is locked. He's going to have to break it down while crawling on his belly.

4:23 a.m.
To accomplish this difficult task, Johnson must use his tools correctly and employ the strength of his upper body. Muscles in his torso, arms, and hands are doing most of the work.

4:27 a.m.
He gets the door open and feels a tremendous blast of heat from the apartment, even through all his protective clothing.

4:28 a.m.
As Johnson begins to search the apartment, he's worried about what he doesn't hear. The screams have stopped; the victim is probably unconscious. He has to calm any impulse to panic, because he must be very methodical in his search.

4:32 a.m.
It is so smoky in the apartment, Johnson may as well have his eyes closed. He has to navigate this unknown space by touch, his legs and hips pushing him along as he crawls on his stomach.

4:34 a.m.
He finds the victim near a window. She is unconscious, so he and his partner have to push and pull her weight, as well as their own, to get her out of the apartment.

4:35 a.m.
Johnson remembers the path he took into the apartment and now retraces it as he drags the victim. Other members of his company are on the stairs, and they carry her down to the ambulance that is waiting outside.

4:37 a.m.
Johnson is outside the building, watching as other firefighters bring the fire under control. He is very concerned about the woman he pulled from the apartment.

4:41 a.m.
Johnson is relieved to find out the woman has regained consciousness. She will be hospitalized for burns, but she will recover.

4:50 a.m.
As the team loads their gear back into the truck, Johnson feels nauseous, a side effect he's come to expect after the kind of muscular exertion his work requires. He knows it is caused by a build-up of lactic acid in his body.

5:10 a.m.
Back at the firehouse, Johnson begins to relax and realize how tired he is. He's so fatigued he can hardly lift his arms.

Activity

NAME THAT SYSTEM Use the scenario above to identify which systems of the body Firefighter Johnson uses in this emergency situation. Remember that some actions use more than one system, and that all the systems are interconnected. Name all that apply. The body systems are: circulatory, digestive, endocrine, immune, muscular, nervous, respiratory, reproductive, skeletal, and urinary. Which systems don't come into play at all in the scenario? (See Answers on page 32 to find out which systems are not involved.)

PICTURE THIS

THE Inside Story

The human body is one amazing machine. If you were able to look inside with a powerful microscope like scientists can, you'd find a trillion different pieces, in different sizes and shapes, all working together in very efficient ways. What's more, they're all packed into a very small space. Your intestines, for instance, are 26 feet (8 m) long. If you're 5 feet (1.5 m) tall, this means your intestines are five times longer than you are!

Our body's tiny, basic building blocks are cells. Cells with the same job bind together to form a specific type of tissue, such as muscle tissue or skin tissue. Different kinds of tissues make up organs, such as the heart, brain, and lungs. An organ can have one job or more. Organs link to other organs and form a system with a particular purpose. For example, breathing is controlled by the respiratory system, and processing food is taken care of by the digestive system. All of your ten systems—circulatory, digestive, endocrine, immune, muscular, nervous, respiratory, reproductive, skeletal, and urinary—work together keeping you alive.

Here are some very close-up and magnified views of what's inside us. See if you can figure out, from the photos and clues, what they are and what systems they're a part of. You'll find the answers on page 32.

It's a Small World

1. The inside of one of your organs is covered with these structures, called villi.
2. Villi help speed the process of absorption by adding more surface area to the inside of the organ.
3. In this organ, enzymes and juices break down substances into tiny chemicals that can pass through the organ's walls into the bloodstream to nourish cells and give you energy. Which organ is this?

Sound Off

1. You have two of these. Each contains fluid.
2. Each does the same two jobs. The jobs are not similar or related to each other.
3. One job keeps you on balance. The other involves vibrations. Can you name the organ?

Stranded

1. It's made of dead protein, yet it's the fastest growing part of your body.
2. It grows from a hole, part of a follicle, under the skin. The body has about five million of these holes. Live cells are found only at the bottom of the hole, at the root, deep under the skin.
3. In teens and adults, it's found all over the body, except for the lips, soles of the feet, and palms of the hands.
4. It stretches when wet.
5. It usually lies flat, but if you get cold or scared, it can stand straight up. What is it?

Activity

SYSTEM UPGRADE Think about the internal parts of your body and what they do. If you could improve on human biology, what body part or system would you choose, and why? How would you improve or add to its function? Draw a picture of this body part or system and write a paragraph describing what you would like the new version to do.

ALMANAC

BODY BASICS

Food = Fuel

You get energy from the foods you eat, which are mainly carbohydrates, fats, and proteins. The energy different foods give you is measured in calories.

This table from the American Dietetic Association shows the recommended amount of calories per day for girls and boys who are average in height and weight. Use the table to estimate the number of calories you need daily. If you're a very active person, you'll need more calories; if you're a couch potato, you'll need fewer.

Who/Age	Average Weight	Average Height	Recommended Energy (calories per day)
All kids/7-10	62 lbs / 28 kg	4 ft 4 in / 132 cm	2,000
Boys/11-14	99 lbs / 45 kg	5 ft 2 in / 157 cm	2,500
Boys/15-18	146 lbs / 66 kg	5 ft 9 in / 176 cm	3,000
Girls/11-14	101 lbs / 46 kg	5 ft 2 in / 157 cm	2,200
Girls/15-18	121 lbs / 55 kg	5 ft 4 in / 163 cm	2,200

TALL TALES

Until age nine, the average height of boys and girls is pretty much the same. Then, things begin to change. Can you spot the two big growth differences? Can you make any predictions about your own height from the data on this graph?

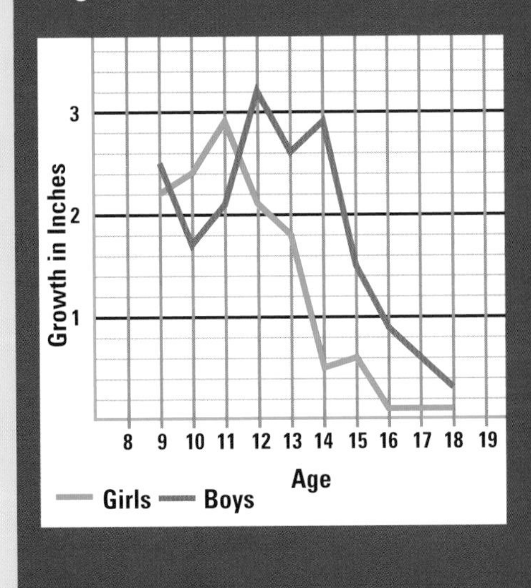

Breakfast Boosters & Bummers

Not all breakfasts are created equal. Compare these nutritional facts for the following breakfast foods. You may already know the bad news about too much saturated fat: It clogs arteries.

Sugar-coated flakes (3/4 cup/1 ounce [28 g])
Calories: 120
Total Fat (g): 0
Saturated Fat (g): 0
Total Sugar (g): 12
Sodium (mg): 150

Wheat flakes (3/4 cup/1 ounce [28 g])
Calories: 90
Total Fat (g): 1
Saturated Fat (g): 0
Total Sugar (g): 5
Sodium (mg): 210

Fruit-filled cereal bar (1.5 ounces [42 g])
Calories: 140
Total Fat (g): 3
Saturated Fat (g): 0.5
Total Sugar (g): 13
Sodium (mg): 110

Scrambled eggs (2, with 1 tablespoon skim milk and cooking spray)
Calories: 173
Total Fat (g): 12
Saturated Fat (g): 3.2
Total Sugar (g): 0
Sodium (mg): 142

Pancakes (4, with 1/4 cup syrup)
Calories: 480
Total Fat (g): 4.5
Saturated Fat (g): 1
Total Sugar (g): 46
Sodium (mg): 625

Source: Nutrition Action Health Letter, November 1999 and the American Egg Board

Cola vs. Cow Juice

"Drink milk, not soda!" You've heard that a thousand times. Yet according to a recent study, teens are drinking twice as much soda pop as milk. Boys ages 12 to 19 drink almost 2 1/2 12-ounce (360-ml) sodas a day. Girls drink more than 1 1/2 sodas a day. Twenty years ago, teens drank twice as much milk as soda.

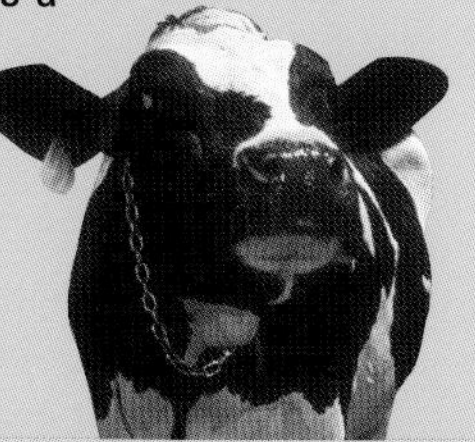

Here's a comparison:

Cola (8 ounces [240 ml])	Skim milk (8 ounces [240 ml])
Calories: 100	Calories: 80
Total fat: 0 g	Total fat: 0 g
Sodium: 35 mg	Sodium: 130 mg
Sugar: 27 g	Sugar: 12 g
Protein: 0	Protein: 8 g
Vitamins: 0	Vitamin A: 10%
	Calcium: 30%
	Vitamin C: 2%
	Vitamin D: 25%

Here's what the differences mean:

Better bones: Milk is loaded with calcium, a mineral needed for strong bones. In the calcium department, soda has zero. Low calcium intake can lead to osteoporosis, a disease that weakens bones. Some soda drinkers consume about 20 percent less calcium than people who don't drink soda.

Needed nutrients: In addition to protein and other nutrients, milk provides vitamins A, C, and D. Soda? None. Many kids are getting 15 to 20 percent of their calories from soda, squeezing out more nutritious foods and beverages.

Tooth decay: Soda bathes your teeth in sugar-water, which can lead to cavities.

Sugar surge: Kids are often hitting their daily recommended sugar limits just by drinking soda. A boy who consumes 2,200 calories of food per day should eat and drink no more than 12 teaspoons of sugar, but the average boy gets 15 teaspoons of sugar per day from soda alone.

Source: Center for Science in the Public Interest, 1998; U.S. Department of Agriculture

Most Teens Don't Smoke

The good news is that most teens don't smoke. The bad news is about 80 percent of adult smokers started smoking as teens. Every day, nearly 3,000 people under age 18 become regular smokers. Tobacco use, however, is the single most preventable cause of death and disease in America. Here are some facts to consider:

- Tobacco smoke contains an estimated 4,000 chemicals.
- Carbon monoxide in cigarettes reduces the amount of oxygen carried in red blood cells by up to 12 percent, making the body work harder to breathe.
- Diseases caused by tobacco lead to more than 430,000 deaths each year in the United States—about one in every five deaths.

Sources: U.S. Department of Health and Human Services; Centers for Disease Control and Prevention; National Institute on Drug Abuse

Activity

ACTIVE TRACK Every person, no matter what age, benefits from being physically active. Physical activity helps keep us strong and healthy. You may be more or less active than you think. Here's an easy way to track how active you really are during one school week. In the box provided in the table below, write the name or type of activity you did for at least 10 to 15 minutes during each 30-minute period. Then record the intensity level of the activity as active, moderate, or light, depending on how tiring the activity was for you. If you were not physically active (you could have been doing homework!), write "rest." Use this table as a model for the rest of the school week. Count up the number of boxes you had in each intensity level.

You're doing great if you did two or more boxes of active or moderate activity for 4 or 5 days. If your total shows 1, 2, or no days of physical activity, you may want to start a new sport or hobby, or maybe try to earn a little money by doing yard work.

Time	Activity	Intensity Level
3:00-3:30 P.M.		
3:30-4:00 P.M.		
4:00-4:30 P.M.		
4:30-5:00 P.M.		
5:00-5:30 P.M.		
5:30-6:00 P.M.		
6:00-6:30 P.M.		

INTO THIN AIR

Jon Krakauer set out in the spring of 1996 to accomplish a lifelong dream of climbing to the top of Mount Everest, the tallest mountain in the world. Battling oxygen deprivation and sub-zero temperatures, Krakauer and five teammates reached the 29,028-foot (8,848-m) Himalayan summit. Tragically, four members of his team and five climbers from other expeditions were killed in a brutal storm that unexpectedly rolled in just as the climbers were beginning their descent. Krakauer survived and wrote a book, *Into Thin Air*, to tell the stirring tale. These excerpts describe his fight against the elements and the special, sometimes excruciating, challenges to his body, on the way up the mountain. (Editorial comments and explanations are in brackets.)

April 28, 1996: Camp Three, 23,400 ft. (7,132 m)

Shining my headlamp on a dime-store thermometer clipped to the parka I'd been using as a pillow, I saw that the temperature inside the cramped two-person tent was seven degrees below zero . . . During the night, our fetid [foul-smelling] exhalations had condensed on the tent fabric to form a fragile, interior sheath of hoarfrost [frozen dew]; as I sat up and began rooting around in the dark for my clothing, it was impossible not to brush against the low nylon walls, and every time I did so it instigated a blizzard inside the tent, covering everything with ice crystals. Shivering hard, I zipped my body into three layers of fuzzy polypropylene pile underwear and an outer shell of windproof nylon, then pulled my clunky plastic boots on. Yanking the laces tight made me wince in pain; for the past two weeks the condition of my cracked, bleeding fingertips had been steadily deteriorating in the cold air. [Fingertips and toes get the coldest because of their small size. They don't have large blood vessels, and in cold temperatures, less blood circulates through these extremities, making them much colder.]

April 29, 1996: Camp Three, 23,400 ft. (7,132 m)

It was late morning by the time I finally [got] into Camp Three: a trio of small yellow tents . . . on a platform that had been hewn from the icy slope by our Sherpas [local guides]. When I arrived, Lhakpa Chhiri and Arita were still hard at work on a platform for a fourth tent, so I took off my pack and helped them chop. At 24,000 feet (7,315 m), I could manage only seven or eight blows of my ice ax before having to pause for more than a minute to catch my breath. . . .

As the afternoon wore on, I began to feel woozy from the fierce solar radiation—at least I hoped it was the heat that was making me stupid, and not the onset of cerebral edema. High Altitude Cerebral Edema (HACE) is less common than High Altitude Pulmonary Edema (HAPE), but it tends to be even more deadly. A baffling ailment, HACE occurs when fluid leaks from oxygen-starved cerebral blood vessels, causing severe swelling of the brain, and it can strike with little or no warning. As pressure builds inside the skull, motor and mental skills deteriorate with alarming speed—typically within a few hours or less—and often without the victim even noticing the change. . . .

May 8, 1996: Camp Three, 23,400 ft. (7,132 m)

[After spending two nights at Camp Three to adjust to the oxygen-thin air, the expedition descended to Base Camp, at 17,600 feet (5, 365 m), to gather their strength for the summit push. Then they returned to Camp Three.]

As darkness enveloped the camp, our guides handed out oxygen canisters, regulators, and masks to everyone: for the remainder of the climb we would be breathing compressed gas . . . .

[I]n the so-called Death Zone above 25,000 feet (7,620 m), without supplemental oxygen the body is vastly more vulnerable to HAPE and HACE, hypothermia [dangerously low body temperature], frostbite, and a host of other mortal perils.

May 10, 1996: Camp Four, 27,600 ft. (8,412 m) and Summit 29,028 ft (8,848 m)

Bottled oxygen does not make the top of Everest feel like sea level. Climbing above the South Summit with my regulator delivering just under two liters of oxygen per minute, I had to stop and draw three or four lungfuls of air after each ponderous step—and this was the fastest pace I could manage. . . .29,000 feet (8,840 m) with gas felt like approximately 26,000 feet (7,925 m) without gas. But the bottled oxygen conferred other benefits that weren't so easily quantified.

Climbing along the blade of the summit ridge, sucking gas into my ragged lungs, I enjoyed a strange, unwarranted sense of calm. . . . I had to remind myself over and over that there was 7,000 feet (2,130 m) of sky on either side, that everything was at stake here, that I would pay for a single bungled step with my life. . . .

Reaching the top of Everest is supposed to trigger a surge of intense elation; against all odds, after all, I had just attained a goal I'd coveted since childhood. But the summit was really only the halfway point. Any impulse I might have felt toward self-congratulation was extinguished by overwhelming apprehension about the long, dangerous descent that lay ahead.

Activity

LUNG POWER Take a deep breath and blow it out. Take another deep breath and blow it into a large balloon, at least 16 inches (40 cm). Tie the balloon off and find its circumference in centimeters. Using your calculator, divide the circumference by 3.14 to get the diameter. Then divide the diameter by 2 to get the radius (R).

Figure out the balloon's volume with this formula: $V=4 (3.14) R^3/3$ (four times pi times the radius raised to the third power, all divided by three). This is your lung volume. Practice and see if you can increase it.

Gotta Have Heart!

Heart Throb

Clench your hand and make a fist. That fist is about the size of your heart! Not very big, is it? Yet this powerhouse of muscle beats about 70 times a minute to keep your blood flowing through your body, all day long, every day of your life. Try squeezing and relaxing your fist that many times in a minute, and you'll have an idea of just how hard your heart works! Squeeze a tennis ball with your hand at this rate, and you'll have an even better idea. Phew!

The heart's job is to pump blood rich with oxygen and nutrients into your blood vessels. The blood delivers these materials to your body's cells, then flows back to the heart. It's pumped to the lungs for refueling with oxygen, then the blood returns to the heart to be pumped through the body once again.

A heart beats about 2.5 billion times in the course of an average lifetime. In just one day, your heart pumps 1,500 to 3,000 gallons (5,625 to 11,250 l) of blood. That blood travels through hundreds of miles of blood vessels. If all the veins, arteries, and capillaries in your body were laid end to end, they'd wrap around the earth twice!

Blood Red

Arteries carry oxygen in the blood away from the heart. Veins carry blood that needs oxygen toward the heart. Blood is red because of an iron-containing red molecule, called hemoglobin, that's in all red blood cells. Oxygen clings easily to hemoglobin. How red our blood is depends on the amount of oxygen in it at the time. Bright red blood has a lot of oxygen in it. The blood in your arteries is bright red because it's carrying oxygen from your lungs to cells around your body. Dark red blood has less oxygen. The blood in your veins is dark red because it has already delivered its oxygen to your body's cells and is returning to your lungs for more.

It's a Nonstop Trip

In 1628, the English doctor William Harvey startled the world of medicine by discovering that blood flows in a continuous loop around the body. Harvey weighed the amount of blood a human heart can hold (about 2 ounces [57 ml]), and then multiplied this by the number of heartbeats in a day. His answer showed that more blood went through the heart than could fit in the body; therefore the same blood must be going through the heart over and over again.

Harvey proved the heart is a pump that pushes blood through arteries, and that blood makes a round trip through the body, flowing back to the heart through the veins. Harvey discovered circulation as well as the heart's real job.

In the Right Vein

We haven't always known that the heart is a pump, or that arteries and veins carry blood. The ancient Greek doctor Hippocrates, who lived from 460–377 B.C., thought blood vessels carried air around the body. The word *artery* means "carrier of air." Hippocrates couldn't study human organs because people used to think it was wrong to cut into the bodies of dead people, even if what doctors learned from dissecting them could help save the lives of others. So Hippocrates and other doctors could only observe the body at work or dissect parts of animals.

More than 500 years later, Claudius Galen, a Greek doctor who moved to Rome in A.D. 162, determined that blood vessels carry only blood, not air. Galen based his conclusions on what he had learned about the inner workings of the human body while treating the many injuries of students at a gladiator school. He also studied how animal hearts and blood vessels fit together.

Galen, however, also had some very wrong ideas about the heart. He thought air in our lungs contained a magical energy that was carried by the blood in liquid form. He thought the liver made blood, and that the heart heated it up. Tiny holes in the heart, he claimed, let blood mix inside it. Blood got around the body by sloshing back and forth in the arteries and veins like tides in the ocean.

Galen's ideas ruled medicine for the next 1,400 years. In 1543, Andreas Vesalius, who taught anatomy in Italy, published an important book based on his studies of cadavers, or dead bodies, that disproved some of Galen's ideas. For example, Vesalius described how he probed the inside wall of a heart with bristles to find the tiny holes that Galen had said were there. He didn't find any.

Galen

Leaf Relief

In the past, people believed that a plant with heart-shaped leaves must be good for the heart. Medicines were made from plants like the violet, which was also called "hearts-ease," and wild ginger, also known as "heart-leaf." The plant that actually helps treat heart disease looks nothing like a Valentine heart. It's called foxglove, and the heart medicine digitalis is made from its dried leaves. This medicine must be prescribed by a doctor, because taking too big a dose can be fatal.

foxglove

Activity

Keep the Beat This box-and-whisker graph shows the range and median of pulse rates for 50 adults while at rest and after 5 minutes on an exercise bicycle.

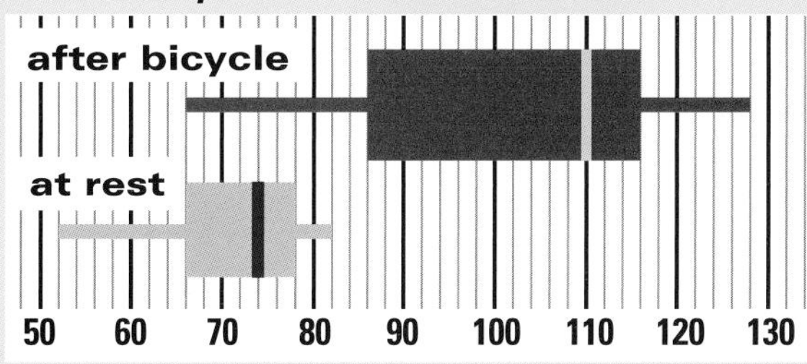

Why do you suppose the range was greater after exercise? Why do you suppose half of the adults had "at rest" pulse rates above the average of 72 beats per minute? Find the "at rest" pulse rates for your classmates. Then check their pulse rates after 2 to 3 minutes of jumping. Create box-and-whisker plots to report this data. Is your class median above or below the "average" rate of 72? What is the mean rate for your class?

All Systems Go

Many people like to challenge their bodies to defeat the physical obstacles of the world, just to see if they can do it. Sometimes this means walking or running faster than the last time, swimming more laps than before, or hiking all the way to the top of a mountain.

Some of these people have performed amazing feats of strength and endurance. You'll find examples of these people on this map. They had to train, practice, and be determined to reach their goals.

Long Distance—Tegla Loroupe, from Kenya, set the world's marathon record for women in 1998. The 1999 winner of the New York City Marathon, Joseph Chebet, was also Kenyan.

NORTH AMERICA

New Depths—The deepest dives happened in Mexico. In 1996, Pipin Ferreras reached 428 feet (130 m) in a breathhold dive. In 1994, Jim Bowden went beyond 925 feet (282 m) in a scuba dive.

Row your Boat—In 1999, American Tori Murden rowed alone across the Atlantic Ocean in 81 days. She is both the first American and the first woman to row across an ocean by herself.

SOUTH AMERICA

All Wet—In 1979, Marcus Hooper prevailed against punishing currents and 60° F (15.5° C) water to become the youngest person to swim the English Channel. He was 12 years old.

Girl Power—In 1999, a 20-year-old Chinese powerlifter named Chen Yanqing, hoisted 290 pounds (132 kilograms) to set a record in her weight class.

Wheel Man—Swiss sportsman Franz Nietlispach holds the world record in the 1,500-meter (.9-mile) wheelchair race. His record time is just over three minutes.

Tour de Lance — American Lance Armstrong won the 1999 Tour de France, the world's most grueling bicycle race. He dedicated his victory to all people who, like himself, have battled cancer.

Everest Ready—In 1997, Tashi Wangchuk Tenzing became the third generation of his family to scale Mt. Everest, the world's highest mountain.

Walk this Way—In 1977, at age 16, Australian Bill Dyer walked 100 miles (160 km) in less than 24 hours, making him the youngest person in the world to become an Australian Centurion.

Snow Going—Boerge Ousland is the first person to cross icy Antarctica alone. In 1997, he made the trek in 64 days, using skis and a sail so the wind could push him along.

Activity

TRAINING SYSTEM Select a person or an activity from the ones shown on this map. Do some research about the kind of training necessary for the activity. Which body systems do you think are most involved in the training? Why? How does physical training specifically affect the body's systems? Imagine you're a news reporter. Write a feature story for the paper's physical fitness section describing the impact training has on three systems of the human body.

Dream On

You've done your homework and brushed and flossed your teeth. Yawning, you turn off the lights, crawl into bed, and close your eyes. Slowly your thoughts become disconnected. You begin to relax. After about fifteen minutes, you're asleep. The next thing you know, it's morning. The whole night seems to have passed in a few quiet seconds. But the night has really been long, full of activity, and far from quiet. Let's turn back the clock and see what really happens after the lights go out.

Twilight Zone

(Stages I and II)

Scientists say there are five stages of sleep, and now, after that first relaxing time, you enter Stage I. You're not yet "sound" asleep; you could be easily awakened by a whisper. Your thoughts become slow and disconnected, and you're getting more and more relaxed. After about half an hour, you're through Stage II. It would take a shout or a shake to wake you up. You're ready for . . .

Deep Sleep

(Stages III and IV)

You're down for the count, in the sweet, refreshing sleep everyone needs to recharge their mind and body. Your muscles are fully relaxed, and your heart rate and blood pressure fall. The electrical activity in your brain slows way down. Now it would take a fire siren to pull you out of this deep, dark, velvet cave. Everyone needs deep sleep, but young people need it for a special reason. It's when an important growth hormone is manufactured. You stay in this peaceful sleep for about twenty to forty minutes. Then you go back to the . . .

Twilight Zone

(Stages I and II)

You may turn over, fuss with your covers, or even open your eyes. Why do you go back to this "partial awakening?" Scientists think it may date back to a time in human evolution when we needed to keep checking for wild animals and other dangers in our surroundings, even while we were getting needed rest. We also need to keep moving so pressure sores don't form on sensitive skin and blood doesn't pool in certain places. It only takes a few minutes to go back into . . .

Deep Sleep

(Stages III and IV)

You stay sound asleep for another twenty to forty minutes. But, now, you're ready for some excitement. Lights! Camera! Action!

REM Sleep

(Stage V)

Your eyes dart around wildly behind their closed lids, giving this stage its name, Rapid Eye Movement, or REM. Your eyes are following the "action" your brain is imagining, the same way they would follow a movie, only you're the one on the big screen of your mind. Your brain is super busy, generating almost the same amount of electricity as when you're awake. But the impulses it's making don't have anywhere to go. Most of your body is frozen, paralyzed. The impulses from your brain are blocked high in the spinal cord, above where the nerves to your large muscles connect. That's a good thing, because, otherwise, the brain could direct you to act out your dreams. Since the nerves to your eyes come from a higher place in the spinal cord, your brain can successfully deliver its message to move. Your pulse keeps time with the action of your dream—getting faster and slowing down—and your breathing and blood pressure follow suit. During this stage, blood flow to your brain dramatically increases.

You're all finished with REM, but the night is still young. You'll go through the entire sleep cycle three to five times this night and most others, with each cycle lasting 90 to 100 minutes. About half of that time will be spent in Stages I and II. The other half will be split between deep sleep and REM sleep. REM will be the final stage before you wake up, which is why some dreams will still be vivid in the morning.

O.K. Now wake up! But it will soon be time for bed again, a special time when, once again, your body proves that even when it's asleep, it's alive.

Activities

Best Rest Having just read "Dream On," you know there's a lot of activity going on inside your body when you're sleeping. Think about the various systems in your body and do some research to find out what your other systems are doing while you're asleep. To start you off, you'll find some clues on these two pages and in "Gray Matters" on pages 6–7. Make a list of your findings.

SCIENTIST'S NOTEBOOK

FROM ART TO HEART

Italy, 1452-1519

If you asked, most people would say art and science have little in common. Art is about drawing or sculpting, while science is about observation, experiments, and conclusions. In fact, art and science are very closely connected—as Leonardo da Vinci knew well.

We know Leonardo best as an Italian Renaissance artist, most famous for his paintings of the Mona Lisa and the Last Supper. Leonardo, though, was an equally talented scientist. Often ahead of his time, he investigated flight, the solar system, and many other scientific ideas.

Leonardo was especially fascinated by the human body and how it works, a curiosity sparked by his art. Which muscles make an arm hang a certain way? How do bones shape a person's face? The more Leonardo knew about the insides of a human body, the better he could paint it from the outside.

But there was not much known about anatomy, or the structure of the human body, in Leonardo's time. So Leonardo studied it himself by dissecting, or taking apart, human corpses and drawing accurate, detailed pictures of what he saw. He sketched close-ups of the larynx and the inner ear; he made cross-sectional drawings showing the stomach and the brain in three dimensions; he mapped the path of blood from the heart through the arteries and veins and back. Leonardo's work gave the world new information about the body. He was among the first to study the womb, to describe the circulatory system, and to investigate the voice.

Leonardo's artist's eye helped his work live on. His drawings of the body—more than 1,000 of them—were so clear and detailed that they are still used in teaching anatomy today. Just as science made Leonardo a better artist, art made him a better scientist.

Houston, Texas, 1966

Doctors and scientists sometimes draw or make models of parts of the human anatomy to better understand how the parts work. Then they can figure out how to repair the parts. Dr. Michael DeBakey made models of the heart and vessels so he could figure out how to mend or replace them.

Dr. DeBakey developed bypass surgery, in which blocked blood vessels in the heart are replaced by healthy vessels from elsewhere in the body. He also invented, and later improved, a machine that temporarily takes over the heart's pumping job, and he built the first artificial heart.

Making new hearts and blood vessels is not simple. In the 1950s and 1960s, many heart specialists doubted it could be done at all. Inventors would have to find materials that would not poison the body, and the artificial devices would need to mimic the workings of the heart to perfection. There was no room for error. There could be no leakage of blood and no skipping or gradual slowing of heartbeats.

Little by little, through ingenuity and perseverance, DeBakey used technology to copy the workings of the circulatory system. He studied how pumps worked, which helped him invent a pump that mimics the pulses of a beating heart. This pump made blood transfusions much simpler. Next, DeBakey created a polyester artificial artery that could replace damaged blood vessels. He bought a yard of fabric and stitched the first model together on his wife's sewing machine. Later, DeBakey built a heart-lung machine that kept the blood full of oxygen, even while circulatory functions were stopped during surgery.

Each breakthrough led to the next. In 1966, DeBakey built a machine called the left ventricular assist device, LVAD for short. The left ventricle is the chamber of the heart that delivers blood to the arteries. A problem in the ventricle affects blood flow throughout the body. The first LVAD implanted in a heart patient kept her alive for ten days, which was long enough for her heart to recover. LVADs were big, bulky, and only temporary solutions to heart problems, but they showed the world that mechanical assist devices could save lives.

Meanwhile, DeBakey designed and built his dream—an artificial heart. But the results were not promising. Technology was not advanced enough to make a successful artificial heart. Even today, artificial hearts do not guarantee long-term survival.

Dr. DeBakey returned to improving LVADs. His most recent model, perfected the year he turned 90, is smaller than a tube of toothpaste and has only one moving part, yet it is more effective than ever. Dr. DeBakey hopes the device can be implanted permanently, helping people with heart problems to live normal lives.

Activity

EYE SPY Artists and scientists are keen observers who see much detail when they are at work. Study the back of your hand. Notice how it bends, where any bumps or ridges are located, and any other features you can see. Draw a picture of your hand in as much detail as you can. Then find a diagram showing the skeletal structure of a hand. What similarities do you see between your drawing and the diagram?

When it comes to repairing the human body, new advances in medical science seem like the stuff of science fiction. But for those who are injured or sick, such advances are miracles in the making.

Give This Man A Hand

A person on the edge of death is rushed to a hospital, where he dies. Thirteen-and-a-half hours later, the corpse's right hand and forearm are attached to a living person's arm. This isn't the latest version of Frankenstein or a science-fiction movie. It's France in September 1998, and an expert team of surgeons from around the world has just completed the first successful hand transplant.

Now the wait begins. It will be three months before doctors are sure that the patient's body will accept the hand. The first hand transplant, performed in Ecuador in 1964, failed. The patient's body rejected the new hand within two weeks. The current patient will take at least 30 pills a day to prevent a similar rejection, and he will do at least a year of physical therapy to make the hand usable. Even so, he's subject to life-threatening infections and may never gain full use of the hand.

Early the next year, in January 1999, a U.S. medical team performs a similar hand transplant. The patient can pick up thin objects, such as a quarter, from a table, turn door knobs, operate a computer, and even hold hands with his sons. He is invited to use his new hand to toss the first ball at a Philadelphia Phillies' home opener—an honor for any hand, old or new.

Some doctors disapprove of hand transplants because they feel the risks to the patient's life outweigh the benefits of having a new hand. In their view, a hand transplant isn't a lifesaving operation and, therefore, not worth the risks. People who are about to receive a new hand don't agree. They feel the risks are justified by the opportunity of living a more normal life.

Growing New Body Parts

It's hard to believe that the mud-dwelling crayfish is better at anything than a human. But it is. When a crayfish loses a claw, a leg, or even an eye, it simply grows a new one. Humans can't do this—yet!

Scientists in Baltimore, Maryland have shown that a special type of cell found in bone marrow, the soft inner center of bones where our blood cells are made, can transform itself into other kinds of cells—bone cells, cartilage cells, or what the soft, bendable "bone" in your nose is made of, fat cells, and others. When scientists grew these special bone marrow cells, called mesenchymal (pronounced mes-EN-ki-mal) stem cells, in the lab and inserted them into bones as a test, they turned into cells that build bones. When scientists inserted the stem cells into cartilage, they became cartilage cells. This is good news for anyone with an injury or birth defect requiring new bone, tendon, or cartilage.

Other scientists are working with stem cells from other sources, such as the brain and embryos, which can turn into even more types of cells—heart, blood, brain, muscle, nerve, and others. Potentially, these stem cells can repair or restore cells damaged by illness or injury, build new tissue, and, one day, new organs. Perhaps most extraordinary are the brain's neural stem cells. In experiments with sick mice, these stem cells automatically zeroed in on the problem cells in the mice's brains and converted themselves into healthy versions.

All of this work is still very experimental. But, in your lifetime, scientists may figure out how to grow whole new body parts. Crayfish, beware. We're catching up!

Christopher Reeve's whole life comes down to $\frac{1}{8}$ of an inch (.3 cm). That's how little the gap is in his spinal column—and how far the actor who played Superman is from walking, moving his hands, and breathing on his own.

Allergic to horses as a child, Chris never rode until he had to learn how for a movie role. He loved riding, and over the next ten years, competed in many horse shows. During a jumping event in May 1995, his horse suddenly stopped short of a jump, throwing Chris off. He landed on his head. Within seconds, he stopped breathing. Luckily, paramedics got to him in time and saved his life. But Chris is paralyzed from the neck down and can't breathe without the help of a special machine called a ventilator.

Doctors cannot repair Reeve's broken spinal cord or cure his paralysis. But he doesn't let that stop him from working with therapists to keep his body as strong and as healthy as possible for when such miraculous repairs may happen. According to Reeve, "I do it as conditioning for the time when there is regeneration of the nerves of the spinal cord."

Reeve's efforts have resulted in visible progress. He has regained some sensation across his shoulders and lower spine, but he has no control over his bodily functions. He maneuvers around in a wheelchair that he guides by puffing air through a straw. He can now turn his head 70 degrees to each side, and he can breathe on his own for up to half an hour.

Scientists have made progress in understanding more about spinal cords and how they work. They used to think spinal cords could never heal and nerve cells couldn't grow. Medical research now shows that they can.

Activity

A HANDY DECISION Many doctors think hand transplant surgery shouldn't be done because it's so risky to the patient's life. If you lost the use of your hand, would you decide to have this surgery? Use the actual debate that doctors have from the end of "Give This Man A Hand." Write out your reasons, yes or no, and share them with the class.

SOLVE-IT-YOURSELF MYSTERY

Danger on EAGLE PEAK

"We're coming in, folks," called the pilot. "Make sure you're buckled up."

"Finally!" said Naomi with relief, taking one last swig of water from her bottle. She and her five-year-old brother, Michael, had been traveling all day. They had flown from Boston, Massachusetts to Aspen, Colorado in the Rocky Mountains for vacation. Their dad had gone on ahead to get the cabin ready, but their mother had to stay behind because of last-minute business problems. "There's no need for everyone's summer vacation to be delayed," Mom had told Naomi. "I'll join you as soon as I can. Daddy and I know we can trust you to take care of Michael on the flight."

Naomi strained against her seat belt, craning her neck to get a closer look outside. They were coming down into a canyon tucked between red, rocky cliffs. Towering above the whole landscape was a steep mountain. Its slopes were covered with dark green junipers and graceful aspens. Sugary white snow spilled over its peak.

"Eagle Peak," the pilot informed them. "Fourteen thousand feet. Highest mountain around. Best place to spot bald eagles in the country, they say. Best skiing, too—but don't try it in June."

The little boy in the bright yellow t-shirt beside Naomi stopped squirming and peered outside. "How come there's snow when it's summer?"

"Because the mountain is so high that the weather is colder at the top than at the bottom," Naomi explained. "I just read about it in this book." She held up a paperback copy of *Top of the World: Life at High Altitudes.*

The plane touched down gently and rolled to a stop. Naomi and Michael ran to meet their father at the gate. Soon the three were in a Range Rover, bumping over a steep, twisty gravel road, climbing higher and higher. "We're up so high that if we come back here in the winter, we'll be able to ski right out our back door," their dad told them. "Isn't that great?"

Naomi noticed that Michael had become very quiet. "My head hurts," he said. Then he brightened. "Can we go find some eagles?"

"We'll have something to eat when we get home," Dad said with a laugh. "Then you can take a nap. THEN we'll go looking for eagles."

When they reached the cabin, their father discovered he had forgotten to buy peanut butter, Michael's favorite food. Actually, it was about the only thing Michael liked to eat. The little boy was getting crankier by the minute, complaining over and over that his head hurt. Naomi's father put him down for a nap, then left for town to pick up peanut butter. "I shouldn't be more than forty-five minutes. You get settled. There's juice and fruit in the kitchen."

Naomi brought an apple and a bottle of juice into Michael's bedroom, but he seemed to be fast asleep. She drew the shade on the big window and tiptoed out. She put her things away in drawers, munching and sipping as she worked. Then she brought another bottle of juice out on the deck and sank into a chair. She was sleepy, and her own head ached slightly. She dozed off, awaking to see a majestic bird soaring overhead. "An eagle," she exclaimed. "Michael should see this!"

She ran to his room but stopped in alarm at the door. The bed was empty. The window shade was pulled up, and Michael was missing.

Frantically, she searched the cabin, but her brother was nowhere to be seen. Outside again, she scanned the mountainside, shielding her eyes against the setting sun. A speck of bright yellow high up caught her eye. Michael's t-shirt!

She raced up the steep slope, panting, still carrying the half-empty bottle of juice, keeping the small spot of color in view. She had to stop every few minutes to hold onto a tree and catch her breath. Finally, she reached her little brother. He was lying in a small heap on the ground, his eyes open. "I almost caught an eagle," he said in a weak voice. His eyes looked glassy as they tried to focus on her. "What's your name?" He was making no sense! "Why are there spots in the air?"

Naomi was horrified. What was the matter with him? Michael closed his eyes again. She had to do something! But what? She scanned his small body for bruises or cuts but found none. Something she had just read flashed in her mind, something she had read. . . on the plane!

Suddenly, she knew what was wrong. She unscrewed the bottle top and supported her brother's head so he could drink a little. She kept giving him little sips until the bottle was empty. After a few minutes, Michael began to revive. She gathered him up, and they slowly started back down the mountain. When they reached the cabin, he was speaking normally. Naomi gave him a big glass of water to drink. By the time their father returned, he was totally himself again, wolfing down two enormous peanut butter sandwiches and talking about the eagle he had seen from his bedroom window and how he had run outside, trying to catch it.

Can you figure out what happened to Michael? Why was Naomi out of breath? Reread the mystery and use the clue box below.

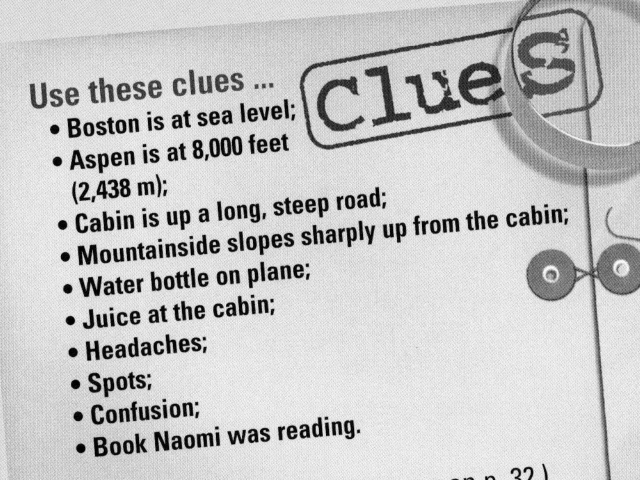

Use these clues ...

- **Boston is at sea level;**
- **Aspen is at 8,000 feet (2,438 m);**
- **Cabin is up a long, steep road;**
- **Mountainside slopes sharply up from the cabin;**
- **Water bottle on plane;**
- **Juice at the cabin;**
- **Headaches;**
- **Spots;**
- **Confusion;**
- **Book Naomi was reading.**

(Based on a true story. Answer on p. 32.)

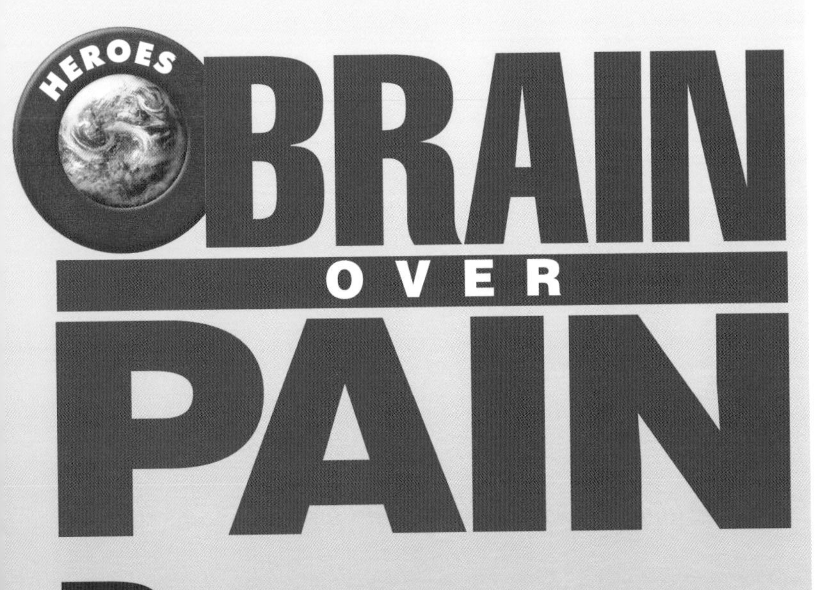

Brain over Pain

Did you know that you can slow your heartbeat by using your mind? That, to a point, you can think yourself sick, or think yourself well? The human body and mind are very closely connected.

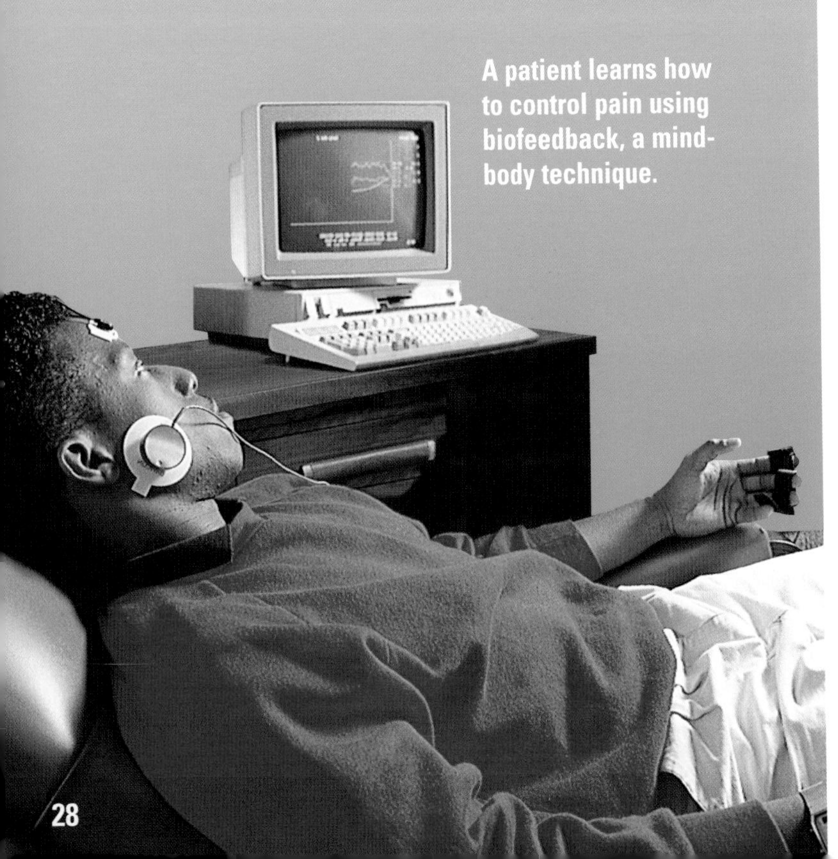

A patient learns how to control pain using biofeedback, a mind-body technique.

Dr. Karen Olness

Mika was a ten-year-old girl who suffered from severe migraine headaches. Medication did not help. So Dr. Karen Olness, an Ohio pediatrician and scientist, tried something different—a mind-body technique called biofeedback.

Olness set up a computer to measure electrical activity in her patient's hands. As people become more relaxed, the electrical patterns in their skin change. Mika could see these changes on the computer screen.

By looking at the screen, Mika learned how to tell when she was relaxed and, then, how to change the image on the screen. For Mika, the key was thinking about tennis. When she imagined herself playing tennis, she became relaxed, and the image on the screen got smaller. Over time, Mika learned to use her thoughts to relax herself more and more, and her headaches greatly diminished.

Olness's work with biofeedback has helped many other children cope with pain and stress. Recently, she collaborated with computer engineers to develop a biofeedback CD-ROM that children can use on home computers.

"It would be wonderful," says Olness, "if every child, beginning at age six or seven, could have the opportunity to be hooked up to a biofeedback system. Then, early on, they would have the experience, 'Aha! I change my thinking, and my body changes.'"

Olness practices what she teaches. She taught herself how to control pain, and her practice came in very useful after a skiing accident. During a 45-minute operation to repair a torn ligament, she focused her thoughts on a very pleasant image—lying in the grass on the farm where she grew up. The technique succeeded; she had the surgery without anesthesia.

Like biofeedback, meditation is a relaxation technique that can be used to help heal the body. Meditation usually involves silently repeating a sound and focusing your attention back to the sound if other thoughts interrupt your concentration.

To experience meditation for yourself, sit comfortably with your eyes closed. Breathe gently and naturally. Whenever you exhale, silently repeat a word, phrase, or sound. The word *one* is often used. Continue for 10 to 20 minutes. If you start thinking of other things, don't let it bother you. Simply return to the repetition.

Scientists were once very skeptical about the effects of meditation and other mind-body techniques on health, but research by Dr. Herbert Benson, a pioneer in the field, and others have changed their minds.

Dr. Benson studied monks in Tibet and other people who meditate frequently. He discovered that meditation slows the heart, slows breathing, and reduces the body's use of oxygen. It also has other positive effects. Recent studies by other scientists confirmed Dr. Benson's findings. Many people who meditate once or twice a day find that it makes them calmer, less stressed, and, sometimes, even more confident. Like biofeedback, meditation can also reduce pain. What this all adds up to is making it easier for the body to function. It doesn't have to work as hard.

Meditation can have many positive effects.

Many people suffer from medical problems caused or made worse by stress, anxiety, and worry. Traditional medicine and surgery don't seem to work well for these people. An astounding 70 to 90 percent of visits to doctors involve this kind of mind-body connection, says Dr. Benson. Dr. Benson is a cardiologist, or heart doctor, and the founder of the Mind/Body Institute in Boston, Massachusetts. More and more, physicians and scientists are finding that biofeedback, meditation, and other mind-body techniques can help people speed the journey to better health.

Activity

BETTER BREATHING "As natural as breathing." That's the expression people use when something is very easy for them to do. But good breathing doesn't come naturally to most people. Michael Grant White is a breathing coach from North Carolina. He works with singers, actors, public speakers, and others to help them breathe better. Good breathing relieves stress, increases energy, and improves performance. Try this exercise yourself, White suggests. Use a partner to read the instructions to you the first few times.

- **Sit erect but relaxed, cross your hands, and place them just above your waist.**
- **Close your eyes. Observe your effortless breathing, and notice how it feels to be breathing in...out...in...out. Do not actively change your breathing. Just sense and observe.**
- **After three effortless in-and-out breaths, let all of your breath out without forcing it. At the bottom of the exhale, press on your ribs by hugging or squeezing yourself. Make a vigorous, loud "shhhhhh" sound to help push out more air.**
- **When you feel that you must breathe in, let the breath come in all by itself. Did a bigger, deeper, easier breath come in?**
- **Wait three effortless breaths, and repeat the process. Start over as often as you wish. Stop if you feel dizzy or have any discomfort.**
- **Do you feel better? More relaxed? More energetic? Do this exercise for several weeks and keep a journal of what and how you feel.**

FUN & FANTASTIC

Body Life

It's a Gas

It's embarrassing, whether it's silent or noisy. You hope against hope it's not the smelly kind. But, then, you smell it. As it spreads through the air, you can see the telltale signs of recognition. Heads move slightly as noses twitch, sniffing a whiff. Then heads turn to identify the culprit. You try to look normal. The smell gets fainter and fades away.

It's happened to all of us. Food we've eaten doesn't get digested—broken down into the tiny molecules our bodies can use—by the stomach or small intestine. Instead, it passes along the digestive tract to the large intestine. There, the food is broken down by bacteria, which produce a bunch of gases as part of the process. Most of the gases, most of the time, are absorbed by the large intestine. When they aren't, they're expelled. The smelly gas is hydrogen sulfide.

From the Heart

People in ancient cultures considered the heart the center of love, bravery, feelings, and thought. Today, we still use many words that link the heart with love, courage, and emotions. A very sad person is "heartbroken" or "heartsick." A cruel person is said to be "heartless." Something that makes you feel good is "heartwarming." You fall in love with a "sweetheart" or a "heartthrob" and you may have a "heart-to-heart" conversation with that person.

In a Word

Can you list the names of 10 body parts that are only three letters long? Here's a hint: five are above your neck and five are below. If you get seven or more, you're doing great!

Answers on page 32.

Figure Eight

Many ladies in the 1800s wore corsets, or stiff undergarments that tightly squeezed in the waist, giving the ladies figure-eight, or hourglass, shapes. In those days, ladies fainted often, and people concluded females were very delicate. The truth is the tight corsets prevented the muscle under the lungs, called the diaphragm, from moving up and down properly. When the diaphragm moves down, the lungs expand to take in oxygen; when it moves up, the lungs return to their usual size and expel carbon dioxide. Corsets prevented the ladies from breathing in enough oxygen. No wonder they fainted!

RUNNING WILD

Don't try to race a grizzly or a rabbit. A grizzly bear can run at 30 miles per hour (48 kmh), and a rabbit scampers at 35 mph (56 kmh). Humans can't run faster than 28 mph (45 kmh). What's no surprise is that we can outrun an elephant—but only by 3 mph (5 kmh). Surprisingly, we're more than twice as fast as squirrels. They dash at 12 mph (19 kmh).

FUNNY BONE

Ever bang your elbow, hitting your funny bone? If you have, then you know it's not funny. Those prickly sensations hurt. What is funny is that you don't have a funny bone. No one does. What hurts is the nerve that's been pinched by the impact of your elbow against the object it hit. That nerve is next to a bone called the humerus.

Sweet Tooth

Your tongue has about 9,000 to 10,000 taste buds that can recognize about 500 different tastes.

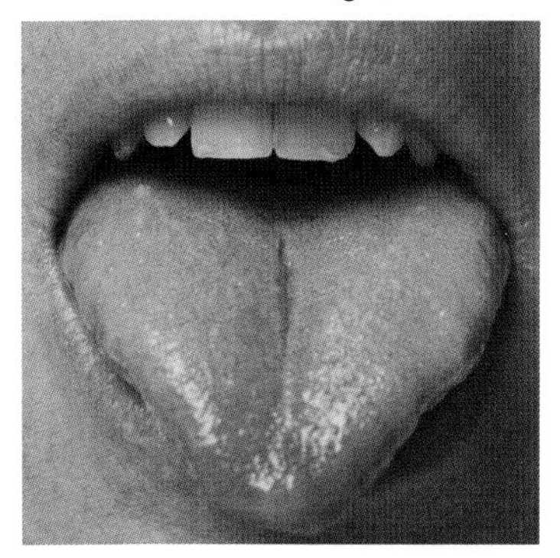

They're closely packed. The taste buds that send sweet signals to your brain are located at the tongue's tip. So, your "sweet tooth" is really your tongue!

BODY BOGGLERS

- **Your fingernails grow about 1½ inches (3.8 cm) a year. That's much faster than your toenails, which grow about one-third as fast. If you're right-handed, the nails on that hand grow faster than the ones on your left hand. The reverse is true for left-handers. Do you know why? See answer on page 32.**
- **A person's head has about 100,000 hairs on it. Blondes have 140,000, redheads have 90,000, and brunettes are in-between.**
- **The right lung is shorter than the left by 1 inch (2.5 cm), but its total capacity is greater because it has three sections, called lobes. The left lung has only two.**
- **Most people can identify 4,000 different kinds of smells.**
- **There are 206 bones in your body but 650 muscles.**
- **You breathe in about 23,000 times a day.**
- **You can't sneeze with your eyes open. The speed of the air down your nose forces your eyes to close. Some sneezes have been clocked at 100 mph (160 kmh)!**

YOUR TURN

In 1513, Spanish explorer Ponce de Leon sailed in search of the Fountain of Youth. He discovered Florida but never found the fountain. Now, nearly 500 years later, a team of scientists may have accidentally stumbled upon it—a gene that seems to control aging. The gene was in a mouse, but the scientists think humans have the same, or a similar, gene. When scientists stopped this gene from doing its job of destroying cells, the mouse lived 30 percent longer and didn't show the usual signs of aging.

When it's your world and your turn, you may be able to live 100 years or longer and be in good health and look decades younger, too.

What would you do with the extra years? Would you continue working at the same job or switch to something else? If you didn't work, what would you do? Would you have enough money to live all those extra years? Would you plan your whole life differently if you knew you would live longer? How would living longer affect your own family? What effect would people living longer have on the planet? Think about the availability of food, space to live, demand on doctors and hospitals. What changes, if any, would you see if there were many more older people alive? Which biological systems would be most affected?

Imagine it is the year 2050 and you are grown up with a family of your own. Government officials are studying the pros and cons of a longer lifespan, and they want to hear what their citizens think. As your final project, write a letter to Gene Centurion, head of the government's research commission, giving your opinions. Consider the questions below:

- In your letter, describe how a longer lifespan could affect you and your body's systems.
- State the reasons for your opinions and include how you personally, the country, and the planet will—or will not—benefit if you and others live 25 years longer.

ANSWERS: Timeline, p. 9

Firefighter Johnson's reproductive and urinary systems are not used.

Picture This, pp. 10–11

A. It's a Small World: The small intestine, part of the digestive system. The photo shows the villi lining the inside of the duodenum, the first section of the small intestine.
B. Sound Off: The inner ear, part of the nervous system. One of its jobs is to change sound vibrations into electrical nerve impulses and send them to the brain, enabling you to hear. Its other job is to keep you balanced. Say you're doing a cartwheel. If the level of the inner ear's fluid tips, nerves in the liquid will send electrical impulses to the brain. You may either fall or be able to regain your balance, depending on how tippy you were.
C. Stranded: A hair. Hair is part of your skin, which is part of the immune system. The immune system helps defend your body against germs. Your skin and hair are your body's outer protective layer.

Solve-It-Yourself Mystery, pp. 26–27

Michael was suffering from high altitude sickness, a condition that commonly affects mountain climbers and anyone else who quickly gains a dramatic amount of altitude, especially when they reach levels above 8,000 feet (2,438 m). In one day, the kids had gone from Boston, which is at sea level, to Aspen, which is more than 1.5 miles (2.4 km) higher. Then they climbed even higher on the drive up to the cabin, gaining even more altitude. Symptoms of high altitude sickness are disorientation, headache, fatigue, breathlessness, and spots in front of your eyes. It can also affect sleep patterns. Why does it happen? At high altitudes, the air is thinner. You take in less oxygen per breath, so there's less circulating through your blood vessels into your organs, causing fatigue and aches. Your heart and lungs start working extra hard as they try to deliver more oxygen to your organs. The air is drier, so you lose more body fluids through evaporation, making you dehydrated. That's why you need to keep taking in fluids. Naomi had water on the plane and juice at the cabin, which is one reason she wasn't as sick as Michael. The juice and water she gave him helped rehydrate him. Another good thing she did was to descend to a lower altitude as soon as Michael was strong enough to walk. These are the first rules climbers learn about dealing with altitude sickness.

Fun & Fantastic, pp. 30–31

In a Word: ear, eye, gum, jaw, lip, arm, hip, leg, rib, toe.

Body Bogglers: Your dominant hand is more active, requiring more blood and nutrients to flow to it. The more nutrients that flow, the more the nails grow.